This Is My Pet!

Helen Chapman

Contents

Odd Pets	2
Stick Insect	4
Mini Donkey	6
Ferret	8
Mini Turtle	10
Tarantula	12
Walking Fish	14
Picture Index	16

Stick Insect

This is my pet.
She has thin legs.
She looks like a stick.

Mini Donkey

This is my pet.
My pet has big ears.
But he is little!

Ferret

This is my pet.
She is long and thin.
She has short legs.

Mini Turtle

This is my pet.
She has a hard shell.
She likes to swim.

Tarantula

This is my pet.
He has lots of legs.
He has mice for dinner!

Walking Fish

This is my pet.
My pet looks like a fish.
But he can walk on land!

Picture Index

ferret   8–9

mini donkey   6–7

mini turtle   10–11

stick insect   4–5

tarantula   12–13

walking fish   14–15